PHJC

I AM A POLAR BEAR

Steve Macleod

MEDIA ENHANCED BOOKS
AV2 BY WEIGL
ADDED VALUE · AUDIO VISUAL

www.av2books.com

Go to **www.av2books.com**, and enter this book's unique code.

BOOK CODE

P755644

AV² by Weigl brings you media enhanced books that support active learning.

AV² provides enriched content that supplements and complements this book. Weigl's AV² books strive to create inspired learning and engage young minds in a total learning experience.

Your AV² Media Enhanced books come alive with...

Audio
Listen to sections of the book read aloud.

Video
Watch informative video clips.

Embedded Weblinks
Gain additional information for research.

Try This!
Complete activities and hands-on experiments.

Key Words
Study vocabulary, and complete a matching word activity.

Quizzes
Test your knowledge.

Slide Show
View images and captions, and prepare a presentation.

... and much, much more!

Published by AV² by Weigl
350 5th Avenue, 59th Floor New York, NY 10118
Website: www.av2books.com www.weigl.com

Macleod, Steve.
Polar Bear / Steve Macleod.
     p. cm. -- (I am)
  ISBN 978-1-61690-759-4 (hardcover : alk. paper) -- ISBN 978-1-61690-852-2 (softcover : alk. paper)
  1. Polar Bear--Juvenile literature. I. Title.
  QL737.C27M24 2011
  599.786--dc22
                                   2010052412

Printed in the United States of America in North Mankato, Minnesota
1 2 3 4 5 6 7 8 9 0 15 14 13 12 11

052011
WEP37500

Project Coordinator: Aaron Carr
Art Director: Terry Paulhus

Weigl acknowledges Getty Images as the primary image supplier for this title.

I AM A POLAR BEAR

In this book, I will teach you about

- **myself**

- **my food**

- **my home**

- **my family**

and much more!

I am a polar bear.

I am one of the
biggest bears
in the world.

I am the size of a kitten when I am born.

I can eat up to 100 pounds
of food in a meal.

I can smell food from 20 miles away.

12

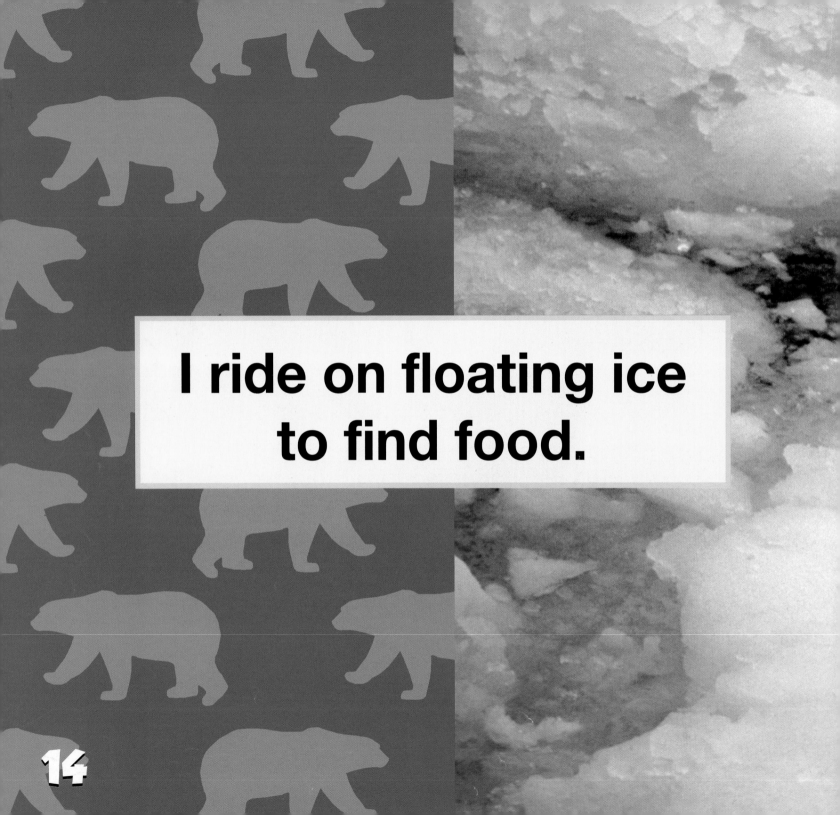

I ride on floating ice
to find food.

14

I have big paws that work like snowshoes.

17

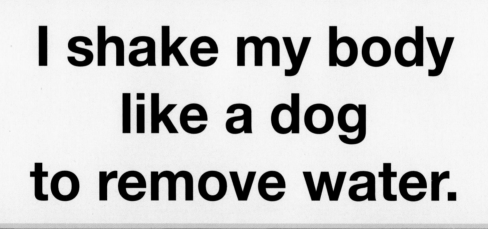

I shake my body
like a dog
to remove water.

18

I live in one of the coldest parts of the world.

I am a polar bear.

POLAR BEAR FACTS

This page provides more detail about the interesting facts found in the book. Simply look for the corresponding page number to match the fact.

Pages 4-5

I am a polar bear. Polar bears have large bodies covered in white fur. They have a long neck with a small head, small and round ears, and a short tail. Underneath their fur, polar bears have black skin.

Pages 6–7

Polar bears are one of the biggest bears in the world. The average male polar bear grows to about 5.3 feet (1.6 meters) tall and 8 feet (2.5 m) long. The heaviest polar bear ever recorded was 2,209 pounds (803 kilograms). That is about the size of a car.

Pages 8–9

Polar bears are the size of a kitten when they are born. Polar bear babies weigh about 1 pound (0.45 kg) when they are born. At birth, these tiny bears cannot see or hear, and have no teeth.

Pages 10–11

Polar bears eat up to 100 pounds (45 kg) of food in a meal. It would take about 300 medium-sized apples to equal that much food. Seals are a polar bear's favorite food. Polar bears also eat fish, ducks, other small animals, and whales.

Pages 12–13

Polar bears can smell food from 20 miles (32 km) away. That is more than the length of 350 football fields or 400 city blocks. Polar bears use their good sense of smell to hunt for food on land and underwater.

Pages 14–15

Polar bears ride on floating ice to find food. Polar bears travel long distances to find food. Although polar bears are good swimmers, sometimes they use pieces of floating ice like boats to cross large sections of the ocean.

Pages 16–17

Polar bears have big paws that work like snowshoes. These paws are 12 inches (30 centimeters) across. The large size of polar bear paws keeps the bear from sinking into the snow. Polar bears also have rough skin on the bottom of their feet, so they do not slip on the ice.

Pages 18–19

Polar bears shake their body like a dog to remove water. After swimming, this helps the fur dry faster. A polar bear actually has two layers of fur. Both layers have an oily coating to help keep water away from the polar bear's skin. This helps keep polar bears warm.

Pages 20–21

Polar bears live in one of the coldest parts of the world. They live near the North Pole. Many scientists believe Earth is getting warmer, causing the Arctic ice to melt. Polar bears are now considered a threatened species. There are fewer than 25,000 left in the world.

WORD LIST

Research has shown that as much as 65 percent of all written material published in English is made up of 300 words. These 300 words cannot be taught using pictures or learned by sounding them out. They must be recognized by sight. This book contains 29 common sight words to help young readers improve their reading fluency and comprehension. This book also teaches young readers several important content words, such as proper nouns. These words are paired with pictures to aid in learning and improve understanding.

Page	Sight Words
4	a, am, I
6	am, big, I, in, one, of, the
8	a, am, I, of, the, when
10	a, can, eat, food, I, in, of, to, up
12	away, can, food, from, I
14	find, food, I, on, ride, to
16	big, have, I, like, that, work
18	a, dog, I, like, my, to, water
20	a, am, cold, I, in, live, of, one, part, the

Page	Content Words
4	polar bear
6	bear, world
8	born, kitten, size
10	meal, pound
12	mile, smell
14	float, ice
16	paw, snowshoe
18	body, remove, shake
20	polar bear, world